I've admired Richard Leigh's poetry for many years: for its honesty, integrity, intelligence and skill. Skill? It's a "no frills" poetry, for none are needed. Yes, but it's still a matter of skill, even if the skill effaces itself, disappears *into* the poetry. I could also say this: it might be seen as bread and water poetry; the best bread, straight from the oven, and excellent water, straight from a cool, clear mountain stream. Add to this his virtues as a translator (and he's also a musician, and has been an editor of note, of the journals *Musics* and *Eonta*). What more could one say, or need to?

David Miller

Anxious Bricolage
RICHARD LEIGH

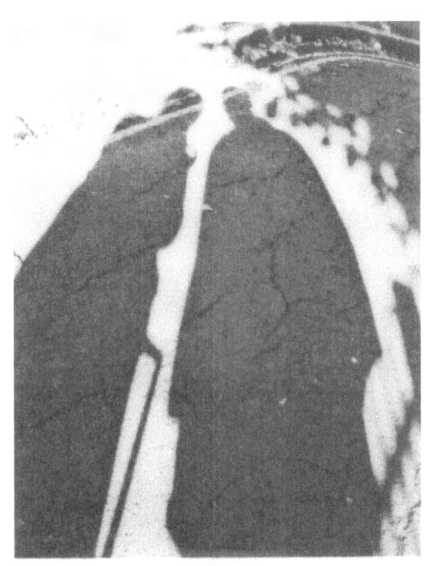

SPUYTEN DUYVIL
New York City

ACKNOWLEDGEMENTS

Some parts of this text have previously been published by Jenny Johnson in "Accidents of Birth" (Nettle Press, 2007) and by David Miller in "Excerpts from MANGANESE" (Kater Murr Press, 2021). I am grateful to both of them for permission to reprint, and for their encouragement over many years, and grateful also to Sheila Beskine for the image used on the cover and title-page.

For Sheila, with love, as always

1

Midway, as good a place

as any

to reconsider
        for example
            unaccustomed angles,
or those neglected corners
            where dust
accumulates,
        and that to no real purpose
            except, perhaps, its own.

Agreed? Don't ask me how I know:
        the shape alone might show you,
            among other things,

the way it seems
        to slope
    as if in partial reply
        to twigs outlined,
cranial, against low cloud.

2

Tentative
    but for each phrase
        the keys just so

as if the years don't pass
        but stay where they are,
           gathering weight.

Openings
    on further openings,
a swiftly glancing
    recapitulation:

this box of tricks
    again obliged to yield,
        each chord
          a darkening articulation,

each line telling you
    there's no such thing as repetition:

the music coming
  each time it's heard
    from somewhere deeper.

3

To put together
  what will stay
together:

a life's work
  on a single breath

a barely-seen procession
    forever winding
            back
into itself
  in shadow;
      and maybe
the interruptions
  are themselves
the procession,
    something
I knew about
    but couldn't call to mind.

Wherever it was placed
      I'd find myself elsewhere,
          unknowing,
a witness
  to what was different,
marshalling my evidence
      to little or no effect.

4

On a day
    perhaps aeons ago
        but as specific as today

there were certain tragedies
            human or otherwise
which seemed to be
    at one remove
or more than one,
        but only seemed to be:

a building whose very shape
      looked like destruction,
all shadow, its walls
        absorbing sunlight.

No support: just
  a galactic swirl
        underfoot.

5

And so, the dust
          settling
     gently as snow
and with the same result

as it goes about its business
     of taking the edge off things.

The dust reminds us
     that we're not necessarily
               alone in being
transitory; though
     we are perhaps alone
in grumbling so much.

We must listen
          closely
to imagine that we hear it
          settling down
for the night.

6

As we lean into the future
        forgive us our instability.

What has been said until now
        is ancient architecture
crumbling to ruin

and we, self-imprisoned,
                        dream
of staring into the sun,
        bearing the grief
of government in exile:

        offal and refuse
of the spirit-house, those
voices, consumed,
  which might have awaited worship,

those arctic blades of light,
        of ice, canisters
mottled, rust-bound

in the separating air:
an echo
full of holes.

7

The beat of our blood
     is unchanged
throughout
  the most attentive listening;

and noises
    heavy as iron limbs
  are grafted, severed,
        fused once more.

Do we tune up
  to the cangue and manacles,
the cold implements
  of the jailer, and of the generations
    inheriting his empty smile?

After toiling over dead knowledge
    we watch the black dawn rising.

All reckoning is fragile,
telling us:
something
has tried to be.

8

Easy to speak about bells,
    their clang and after-shock
        shaking the brickwork loose.

Less easy to recall
        passing-bells
carrying their freight of fear.

Harder still to talk
    against the uproar
        of the planets
in their struggle to survive.

Perhaps the talk
    over time
      will thin out,
become clear
      translucent, even
        if we can just let it alone
      for long enough;

and we, with our faded
      photographs of phonemes,
         try, in the gathering gloom,
to make out the words
        feebly waving
phantom limbs
    in hail
      or farewell.

9

Feeling frail
    just to think
of who preceded us

feeling provisional
                as though
only a breath
    taken by who knows
at the start of a chorus
    shifting
the vast weight
                back
to origins unknowable

                lowering
into what well
        straining
to raise something
    to the air, to the light

something so brief
    and simple

it should be clear;
    and yet
who knows how, mid-phrase,
    just one
unexpected note
    can so tilt the heart?

10

The gloom
      of solar eclipses:

so sad a place,
         its ghosts
await our pity
        always, perhaps.

However it can be,
        it has to be,
a world
   never quite ours
      though we might try
         to make it so

studying
   in good faith or bad,
trembling a little
   in dread of failure

longing
    for another moment's
knowing,
    but forever
short of it:

Let me work
    just a little longer.

11

It is an interweaving
            beyond, and back again:
the knots
        the unravelling

in this serenity:
reflections, replies
            to no questions asked

lines
    making their peace
one with another; and we?

We have so much to say:
        our gravestones
            will lean together
exchanging epitaphs.

12

Next time, we'll know
        and it could be
next time
we'll be wrong again

because it isn't alchemy
        when the changes
reveal themselves

it isn't alchemy
    because the gold
        was always there
            awaiting its moment

the depths
    being just the flip-side
        of the shallows

the gold itself
        a kind of manganese.

13

That they'd had slaves
                  was obvious;
not that they'd written
                  the evidence.

.

But we dug deep,
                  to regain
the slightest trace.

         Here or there
remnants
         of their buildings:
even the shallowest indentations
                  in ancient mud
                       showing
the paltry dimensions
         of the slaves' quarters:
airless, fetid, functional.

And now
the archaeologists themselves
feel stifled
at the thought of it.

They wish they'd stayed at home.

14

We have found ourselves
                    in cities
whose names
                    change
from one day to the next:
                    strange cities
where we have always lived.

There are many
                    who have yet to hear
the voices
          of their own times;
and time itself?

                    Stagnant,
coloured by decay.

We see our strange cities
          reduced to blood, smoke, rubble.

Like the poor at a soup-kitchen
    we form a queue
        for dreams to be dished out to us;

and after a while
    on our weak shoulders
        we start to feel
the weight of the clouds.

15

We must take dictation
　　as fast as we can:
cartography
　　　　by lightning flashes.

The thunder
　　which can safely be ignored
　　　　　takes note of itself
　　　　　　　and echoes
earlier thunderclaps
　　　like interlinear glosses,
or Chinese whispers;

and something
　　will break through
in spite of our worst intentions,
because
　　we can never know
　　　　the purpose of understanding.

16

By turns, returns
　　whatever speaks
wherever
　　is spoken of

every genius
　　a *genius loci*
hiding its place
　　　　within itself,

a going against
　　easily mistaken
　　　　for forward motion;

the last is shadow,
　　　　the last-but-one
is also shadow,

a punctuation,
　　a body of water
　　　　turning, again.

17

During the steam-and-piston days
         (even the imagining of change
            kept at a distance)

count off the openings
         timed to outlast
mildewed monuments,

to hang
         in the air
for as long as needed
         at the very least;

and the music's after-image,
        off minor,
            a system
of penumbrae
        overlapping, receding,

a gradual wash,
        wash, of sound.

18

The great rose
          shedding
          its multicoloured shadow
on grey slabs:
          the stab
of memory.

          The sky, now,
part-empty;
and a landscape-craving eye.

Cannibal isles,
          towers of blood,
all that tourist cliché.

19

Leaving the battered oratory, turn,
　　　again, turn, above
this city small as a postage-stamp,
　　　　above this museum of acts, hover,

trying to remember,
　　　to remember
to –

　　oblivion
　　　　being set aside
　　　　　a minute at a time.

20

Let tongue taste
        unrewarded,
inconsolable,
        the words
which slide us
        in and out of dreams

and later can't explain
        those lendings and borrowings
                of sense,
a language
    trying to speak to us
        as if a telephone
rang unanswered
        for a thousand years.

21

Silent the site
    of the Old Enclosure.
A nasty aftertaste, freedom
      bartered for empty plaudits,

and *an imputation of tyranny*
    or ostentatious splendour.

Burdened with ice-blocks,
      log-jams,
the salt sea,
     locked tight
in a gesture of submission,

      the stone yacht
rising,
       the iron lawns,
the jungle
    shattered.

22

The lineaments
        can be left safely
                to someone else,
pivot
        of everything:
the maligned and forgotten
        of shanty-towns,
a sound
        made in the mind only,
a first draft
        of humanity,

in the absence of clear instructions,
                taking a sledge-hammer
to demolish a rainbow;

and birdsong
                silenced.

23

Music populates
          the emptiness,

white expanse
          away forever

small noises
          characterising cold

a broken figure
          returns to its magma

spindle, remnant,
               paring of life

the source
               never revisited.

The icon of touch
          unlocks the fixity of need
                    flowing toward, amid.

Pigment speaks:
dream-perspectives
yield up the living.

24

Opening the night
    behind the scenery
        beyond the scattershot,
    the after-image,
      mutability.

Everyone knows
    that change is constant,
      unyielding;

but the shyly proffered
        facsimiles
are nothing
    but calligraphy
sorted by size,
    irrelevant criteria
regardless of the consequences.

25

Waking from incoherence
　　　　　to a vision
of frail armies
　　　　　their shattered panoply
　　　　　turning
to rust
　　　under blinding sunlight

and of edicts handed down:
　　　　　crucial
but beyond comprehension.

　What was, but is not;
what will be, but is not:
　　　barely
the space of a breath.

26

All vision
    is vision in a fog,
a children's song
    or a cluster of bells
their ringing tattered
    by the winds' shifting.

But you
    when we need pause
give us pause; and we,
    longing for warmth,
trying
    to feel at home
in this   immensity,
    fleeing
as best we might
    the loneliness
    of hotels, hospitals,
oil-rigs, prisons,

know that if we ask you now
　　　　it won't be prayer
　　　　but only saying something
so you'll know we're here,
　　　　keeping you in mind.

27

Applaud the requiem:
    still gripped by vertigo
you haven't heard the last,
    and can't distinguish
control
    from the pangs of undergoing.

In the blank darkness
    of unpeopled rest,
dreamwork-machine
    in frenzied disengagement,
worrying at a heap of fragments,
    the names of logic.

Turn from the scattered drift,
    the stars' precision,

peel back the landscape: there,
    sudden
        as blood beneath a stone

the light, once dim
and dusted with cobwebs,
glitters harshly at the eyes.

A sad procession,
the third and last,
has just gone by in silence,
back to its darkness.

28

Quiet now: don't ask me how I know.

Never attempt to learn the cause
                    but now,
            on the bleak prospect
          of that architecture,
its ambiance of power,
                    turn your back.

What we need
      we never learn,
          our days
                squandered on consolation.

We try to read
      the silence of gravel-words,
to hold that image close:

a further questioning
      whose purpose
            remains unclear.

29

It might have taken you further
                each time a little more
                incantatory and elusive,
saying what you had to say,
            though not in so many words:
a Claude-glass held up to history
                hoping to simplify;

and in the darkness
        of the stone caravanserail
you waited for a glimmer
            to guide you to the exit.

Whatever could be,
        was self-explanatory.

Why did you look for a reason,
listening to the locomotive
            as it called
            inconsolably
to its distant mate ?

30

Don't presume
    to find continuity

what's there
    is not for you to say.

Take care: it could be
        nothing but cold
  architectural fantasy,
      a nasty whiff of imposition.

Complicity won't save us
    but only weaken us the more.

And we? Condemned
  to a music which lacks
any sense of strain, we
    go down for the third time
        into a suffocating blandness,
all direction gone.

And so
don't waste your time
waiting for polite enquiry
to shade into inquisition
but quietly
make what escape you can.

31

Don't you know?

They sing
            high
in the trees
  or hiding in hedges:

it is as if,
    it is as if....

a tactile music:
            the fingers
itch and curve to play it
            over,
once again;

        but the birds
        keep their counsel.

32

An intractable magma
        holds it all in place
as if there were one
        and only one.

Remember
    when it all seemed
strange,
    and unaccountable?

You must have thought of it all
        as if in easy installments,
                slowly
turning backward to forward
        and back again,
a fluttering oscillation
    which told you

leave while you still can
    or stay forever.

Now we see
    that the choice was yours,
    as it had always been:
        no choice at all,

so very slowly revealing,
        one layer at a time,
    that you were mired,
pitifully enmeshed,
      and didn't know it.

33

It is a gradual
　　honing and shaping:

take it nice and slow
　　and still it will
for a very long time
　　　　continue
to elude you.

Take it at speed
　　and you'll never know
　　　　what, if anything, hit you.

It should be enough
　　　　　to say
something
　　to the following effect:

that nothing here
　　or anywhere worthwhile
　　　　is about anything

and nothing worthwhile
explains itself
or anything
else.

34

Luckily
　　it isn't always night

sometimes an interval
　　　　　of illumination

Barbados, for example,
　　　　　in bright sunshine

viewed from the boat
　　across glimmering water.

White horses
　　couldn't drag you away;

and the shock
　　　　of rock-salt
sudden on the tongue.

35

Only the lake
  (darkness unfolds, enfolds)

peripheral shadows,
          logic of dream
unpicks
    abandoned meanings

the quicksilver
      running off the mirrors.

He was, and is not:
    memory, a crow hovering,
picking, discarding.

You can see it all at once,
      what was, what will be,
            impacted, impaled, held.

36

Outside, all's bleak and hostile,
    come-uppance
set aside
    once and for all.

Enter your own forgotten kingdom
        or stay outside it
and take your chances
        as if they were not just yours.

The music, off minor,
    all clangour and gavotte,
is relegated to liminal extremes,
    facsimiles of places,
covered in dust;
    though usually, of course,
the opposite occurs
    if anything does.

37

It could be that music
        is made entirely of ideas
which are not in things,
        and none the worse for that;

and it could also be
        that as you awake
            from futile dreams of structure
there's a slow melting
                of the age-old
prison of ice.

38

It is as if
    you say

it is as if

    like some
philosopher-bird
    perched
        perchance
on the curve of a twig

    while the chattering bleep
            of the telegraph
covers enormous spaces
        conveying news
perhaps
    of a person
        or persons
            unknown.

39

Sometimes a phrase
                slowly
lurches on its axis
           never quite over-
              balancing,
          and yet *with a quality*
        of infinite distance

and restores us
            unexpectedly
to an equilibrium
           which we don't think we deserve.

40

Smouldering edges
      of dark and light

shadows derailed:
    the clock-tower, its domain.

Synapses
      rotting, stinking,
memory
   riddled with gaps,
the eyes
     deserted, left
         to their own devices.

41

Misdirections echo, distant responses
thrown back:
a ferocious paraphrase?

You spoke of a stain:
hush, now, or tell
what shape lack takes,
bled to the edge, none;

and have done.

42

So now you
        listen, as
bees knock
        plumply
on window-panes
        and the hills
quietly drift and erode
        while church-song
pours, honey-slow
        over the fields
and their cloud-cast shadows.

Tell it as you hear it:
        it's your errand
    so don't try
sending someone else.

43

Somehow the ears
          teach the body
to sway
                    away
and back, again

the ears
     set the body singing,
a melancholy
          reiterated delicacy

an ugly beauty
     which, somehow,
keeps
          its balance.

44

Do you recall
    the last forlorn
      apparition
of *the master of space*
      and time,
of nuance
    and understatement ?

45

It was a shelter
            you must have built
        before you were born
for yourself
        for all of us:
a sound
        with its inbuilt
                    echo

which nobody needed
        until it was there,

the whispered subterfugue
            of supernovae
            heard
as in the similitude of a dream ?

46

Something tells you
        you're on your own

and at a time
        when danger
might stare you in the face

the usual props
absent, or kicked away,

the outlines are clear
        and regular enough

yet strangely
        off-kilter:

be neither complacent
        nor afraid.

47

And what is handed on?
            Can we know?

We are, after all
      the *transitory poems*

and the bond of listening
          severed, eventually

and I would not revisit
        or admire
after you've gone,
      on your behalf.

The voice
    darkens
with age
   the streets
      cast shadows
on themselves.

48

Those who remember us
         will be forgotten
and there
     will be an end to it.

There will be those
         paid to imagine
what might have been:

         sounds, for example,
like the music of the spheres;

and memory will be
     a thickening mist.

But the logs
     spit and crackle
         in the grate,

the donor and his wife
standing at each side
eternally, it seems,

date and time
known to the minute.

49

There is a joke
        for those with eyes
to hear it

and somehow
 Bird contrived
    to die laughing.

Staring at death's door
   can't you see through it
        to the funny side?

The solemn stagger
        tightrope-walking
                inches from the floor?

50

This is not a place
      where you could wait
for company, forever

squinting perhaps
      through
  the blunt end of a telescope

at ever-diminishing returns,
         gone
into that day-dream
    (a terrifying
        fragmentation)
with nothing
  to be hoped for
        dreaded
  or thought.

51

The tragedy
        of the hopelessly
                outmoded
with a rich lattice
        of aphorism,
                confessional,
yet somehow
        reduced to reticence.

                A hermeneutic
vulture, mantling,
        its wingbeats
                of eternity, its
arcane viewpoint,
        flutters,

                the rest of us
        trying to reckon up
                the ten thousand things
                        factorial!

52

It was is if those boats
                          became
becalmed
                slowly
from hull to hull, those
                          boats
preserved in glassy stillness

                        specific fruit
of this particular
                afternoon.

You glanced
        from time to time
    your forehead
            pressed to the window

out, onto that so slow
                    shifting
    easily,uneasily, easily
                        around
and closing.

53

An unpeopled landscape:
          someone appears
      striding
          toward the edge of the frame
      not expecting
to meet another,
      and no-one is there.

      The candles
(representing whom?)
   are lit one by one

and then the face,
      aged, mild, looks down
as he says
   all my nightmares take place here.

Walking the path, you hear
          something resembling a sigh,
start to run for home,
          say not a word.

54

You are wandering
          through enigmatic fields
                    remote as the Antarctic

where you've gone to forget,
                    mulling over a mess
          of the half-recalled,
                              the half-imagined.

If there were doubt
          would it shade
                    into paranoia,

a thin mist
          of introspection
                    ineluctably thickening
                    to fog?

No-one who followed you,
          wishing themselves elsewhere,
                    could hope to understand.

55

You'd hoped for a field-day
       gleaning the aftermath.

You liked to consider how
       as you lay comfortably
              tucked under the welkin

meaning could turn on a dime
       and what had been seen
              as merely objective

would start again,
       and restart
          in shadow,

far above the eagles' playground,
or the slow
       oscillation
of water-lilies
       on the stream.

56

Your oblique intelligence
    permits a sidelong
        glimpse of elsewhere.

You, on a self-made slope
    telling you when to turn
        or give a little to prevailing winds,

slide, as if easily,
  through miles and years
    of rationale:

muscle-tone warps itself
    gently out of shape
   obeying silent dictates.

Criss-cross, the reference
    back, to darkness:
risk is its own reward.

57

Squint
        at the seemingly
                    inappropriate
grace-notes, the beat
                    appearing
to fall just wrong,

        step back
in order to hear it whole.

What seemed at first
        like someone keeping time
is just the steady
                    drip, drip
        of eternity
draining away
        a minute at a time.

58

Now you see it,
		now (at least at first) you don't
and now

		the puzzlement remains
as though

			seeking exactly
				what had for so long
			been elusive

				you stood on tiptoe
			for a closer look
					at the stars.

Born in 1944, RICHARD LEIGH has been writing seriously since the early 1980s. His previous book was *Accidents of Birth* (2007). He has also been published by the Kater Murr Press as well as Babel, The Honest Ulsterman, The Rialto, Iron Press and others. Leigh's main influences from an early stage were Pound, Gary Snyder and haiku. His poetic heroes are Mandelstam, David Jones and Seferis.